Visions of the Outside World

Visions of the Outside World

Poems

by

Chester Sakamoto

For my Mom and Dad,
for their unwavering faith in me,
and for S, M and B,
without whom

FORWARD

The bulk of these poems was composed under peculiar circumstances under which, not only me, but the entire world found itself. Such circumstances were quite unlike anything we had ever seen or experienced before. Whole cities were shuttered and emptied, becoming ghost towns virtually overnight. Businesses shut down, many, unfortunately, for good, as the world economy was dealt a crushing blow. Hospitals were overrun with the sick and vulnerable and their staffs rallied to the front lines much like troops in a war. The reason for all this? A virus, that most humble of entities which cannot be seen by the naked eye but can be the cause of such destruction and havoc. Several people were affected, both directly and indirectly. Some died. It was a dark and difficult time but, through it all, we tried to make sense of it as best we could.

Most of us retreated within ourselves, questioning the very reality in which we were living, yet making the most of the time by improving ourselves and the things in our immediate surroundings. Some began diet and workout routines. Others took on household projects they had been putting off for years. And some of us started to create. I was of this latter group, who, not being able to travel or see much of the outside world at the time, read books, watched You-Tube videos and even spent several hours on Google Maps and Images exploring this marvelous planet (which I look forward to doing once this clears up entirely), all of which germinated into the volume you now hold in your hands.

But my purpose for compiling this collection is not to necessarily chronicle a specific event inasmuch as it is a hope that I have created something truly universal which can be read and enjoyed no matter the era. Allen Ginsberg once said something to the effect that the poet writes for the time in which he is living. That may be true to an extent, but I personally believe that the best work is timeless and transcends both time and place. I am hoping that I have accomplished that with these simple words and poetic ruminations.

PROLOGUE: THE INVISIBLE ENEMY

The engines of pestilence terraform the planet,
Leaving mayhem in their wake.
The medics,
Overwhelmed by the wounded,
Valiantly take up arms against the monstrosities,
But to no avail.
The monsters' appetite for destruction is insatiable.
What,
If anything,
Will stop them?
Surely not the 'fearless' leaders who sent countless innocents into the fray,
Unprepared,
Or else jeopardized civilian lives due to their flagrant abuse of their own rules.
Hypocrisy at its finest.
It's what drives the seemingly endless conflict forward as the invisible enemy rubs its hands and laughs at us.

Part One: Spring

"Lifeless in appearance, sluggish, dazed spring approaches. They enter the new world naked, cold, uncertain of all, save that they enter."
    --William Carlos Williams, Spring and All

EARTH DAY (MOTHER NATURE VICTORIOUS)

Dolphins return to Venice!
The birds reclaim their empire
over the skies!
The city of Atlantis rises from the depths
in all its gilded splendor!
But where is the celebration?
Where are the revelers come to bask
in such an auspicious occasion?
The silence that sweeps the Earth is loud,
To say the least,
But it proves once more that Mother Nature
always gets her way.

GOD, ABSENT

My soul collapses along the ramparts
of the Holy City.
The diagnosis: spiritual deficiency.
'It occurs quite often in our current age,'
The doctor reassures me,
Waving it off as if it were of no importance.
Meanwhile,
The heavens disintegrate,
Their clouded climes spiraling earthward.
Angels with clipped wings tumble and fall.
The laws of gravity spare no one.
God's throne sits vacant.
Who will take up His mantle?
I shudder to think…

The pavement splits open.
Claw-like hands reach up to greet me.
Forked tongues hiss empty promises
of salvation.

How did it come to this?
Millennia of history and heritage laid to waste
like the ruins of some long-forgotten civilization.
A marble likeness of Moses is smashed to bits.
His divining rod lies broken at his feet.
Is nothing sacred?
The heathen Saracens run amok.
If they had their way,
We'd all be shackled together,
Forced to bow before the idols of Marx and Engels.
The prophetess said,
'There will come soft rains,'
But answer me this: When?

THE NEW ATLANTIS

These are the engineers of old who made
a mockery of Mother Nature,
Building gates and locks to keep the brine
from mingling with their bitter tears.
The village idiot is strapped to a windmill.
He laughs as he spins,
For the velocity drives him further insane.
How dare they bar the philosopher from taking
his eternal rest within the Jewish cemetery.
Your false claims of heresy should only be so
benevolent.
The mad painter has kept his sunflowers on the
windowsill again.
See how they wilt in the Dutch rain.
Vivisection occurs daily at the brewery where
the borderline is vague.
Walloon or Hollander?
Make up your mind.
There are more pressing matters at stake.

UPON SEEING VAN GOGH'S *STARRY NIGHT*

The Earth breathes.
The breeze stirs the leaves
on the trees.

If I could walk all night,
I would.
I'd bound out the front door,
Across the Central Valley,
Through the timber forests
of Oregon,
Past the volcanic peaks up
to French Canada,
Where snow falls in May.

Let us, then,
Usher in a new era,
One where the artist or poet
isn't cast out by society,
But is instead embraced for the
visionary genius he is,
For the appetites of the heart
he whets with his brush or words.

L.A. IMPRESSIONISM

The streets are empty.
My heart beats in time
to a lilting jazz piano as,
Hands in my pockets,
I amble along the sidewalks
I know well.
Neon reflects in my eyes,
But there's no one to behold
its wonder.
In the hollowed-out booths
of cafes,
I can hear the laughter that once
was there.
How it seems ages ago now.
And on the wind,
The hum of phantom traffic
is a reminder of what used to be.
I shed a tear,
Knowing damn well that,
Like so many others,
I took it all for granted.

RHIANNON

Up until a certain age,
All I knew were figments of imagination.
Nothing was real,
And I made it through the ether with as much
tact as possible so that,
When I became a man,
I'd know how differentiate fact from fiction.
Well,
I've finally reached that point.
And you know what?
I still can't tell.
Life is a beautiful illusion.
Her nimble fingers spin an elaborate web
that ensnares us all,
Yet protects our fragile souls from harm.
You know her.
You've seen her as I have.
You run to her now,
Greeting her like an old flame,
A dear friend.

MADONNA AND CHILD

A little girl with a red raincoat and a unicorn umbrella
stands on the corner with her mom.
So assured is she that the mythic beasts will protect her
from the elements.
Their shapeless forms gallop across the canvas in a frenzy,
Manes blowing in the wind.
The singular horn protruding from each forehead acts as
a lightning rod to deflect any incoming strike.
Her mother calls for her.
Holding hands,
They cross the busy intersection,
This Madonna and child,
Whose imagination radiates like the sun.

FINN MACCOOL

Who but a burly giant could burn his finger
On a smoked fish and gain knowledge of everything?
I reflect upon his discoveries over my third pint of plain.
The pub smells of kimchi and foreboding
(Only in the New World can those two things clash)
And the rain on the glass blends the colors of the street together
Like a Monet painting.
Oh, severance!
How does one detach from something so easily?
Perhaps the Buddha was right,
That all suffering is tied to earthly possessions.
We suck at the breast of greatness,
Hoping it'll grant us immortality,
When so many of us fall short.
Where's the hope in that?

But it's not all chaos and despair.
For every negative action,
There's an equal and positive reaction.
That's physics,
The way of all things.
Just ask him.
He who's older than time itself,
Who knew the mountains as they formed
And speaks the language of the heart.

BAYOU COWBOY

He wakes every mornin' with the sun,
Wades in the water an' shoots a gator
Afore bringin' it back to his kin.
'*La famille est le plus important*,'
He says to me,
His Gallic brow furrowed in concern.
From Lake Charles to Pontchartrain,
Notoriety will only get you so far.
I realize what he means
As the truck bounces along the dirt road,
Kicking up a storm of dust behind us.

DRAGONFLY

Praise be to the dragonfly,
Wide-eyed brahmin who sees and knows all.
You spend your days meditating upside-down
on a blade of grass,
Your head turned skyward.
What is it you seek?
A higher plane of existence?
Enlightenment?
Or perhaps your next meal?
Your mysteries beguile us as you chant on leaflike
wings:
'Choose your directions wisely,
For the wheel of karma will soon be turning.'

VIOLENT HAIKUS

Protestors stir the
Flames of anarchy with their
Molotov cocktails.

Police strike back with
Billy clubs raised high over
Their beetle black heads.

Crack! Pow! Crimson stains
On the wall, a Rorschach test
Of insanity.

SLEEP PARALYSIS

The crescent moon smiles at me,
But is it genuine or one of mockery?
Such nagging thoughts so late at night that fill me
with unease.

CACTUS FLOWER

I lick my finger and hold it up to the wind.
A storm's blowing down the Cartesian plane.
So I walk fourteen miles 'til I hit a tavern
Where the patrons are drunk and sing songs
about a generation
That was cheated out of experience by trivial
bullshit.
How much longer must we endure this?
The rain pounds the roof and the top of my skull.
I'm tired and weary.
Oh, how I envy the cactus flower,
Who blooms and dies all in a day,
Not having to worry about life's woes.

WINDSURFING

A crow disembarks from the top of the shuttered cinema,
Which has assumed the silent,
Decrepit majesty of an Ancient Greek amphitheatre.
Catching the wind beneath her wings,
She soars gracefully over the blacktop.
Most would pass her off as an omen of impending doom,
But I know better.
She merely longs to be free,
As we all do.
What I'd give to spread my own wings and take to the skies,
Yet I remain earthbound,
A slave to my species' drab evolution.

VISITING THE ANCESTORS

The names are forever etched in stone,
As if the power of language keeps them alive.
I trace my finger over the ancient characters,
Words only my heart can understand.
So I clasp my hands in prayer
And bow deeply in respect.
The sweet incense is meant to calm me,
But cleanses my spirit instead.

INK

His tattoos read like a book,
The story of his life for all to see.
It's just that some of us are better at reading
between the lines.

EMPIRE OF THE ANTS

They divide themselves into opposing factions:
Brown versus red,
Greeks versus Trojans,
Carrying out their military campaigns as we go
about our daily affairs,
As if the fate of their world means nothing to us,
Paling in comparison to our own concerns.

FEAR AND LOVING IN THE GAMBIA

The man whose eyes were in his hands,
He showed me the way.
Stepping from his hut,
He points eastward sagely,
An enlightened smile on his face.
So it is that I follow the barefoot prophets
from Lake Tanganyika to the Nile River Delta,
Searching all the while for the innocence I've lost.
There's not a corner of God's green earth they
haven't blessed.
It's their sacred duty to keep the cycle of love
going strong,
So that the world will never perish.

APPARITION

Golden hair,
Fair skin,
Light eyes.
Did I imagine it?
Perhaps I fell asleep while watching the climbers,
The afternoon sun hot on my back.
Then who or what was it that woke me,
Stroking my cheek so tenderly?
Perhaps the reeds reached down to tickle my face,
Yet when my eyes opened,
I saw him before me,
A finger pressed to his lips to indicate that no one should hear,
The hawks overhead the only witnesses to two souls becoming one.

THERE SEEMED A RIVER

There seemed a river,

    Upon whose banks Yocheved sent the infant Moses adrift,

    Upon whose shores the first cities arose,

    Upon whose sands the pyramids were built.

The history of humanity has been dependent upon rivers,

    Valuable arteries whose life's blood has stirred our own,

    Inspiring us to create,

    To be one and level with our gods and reach our full potential.

MANSUR'S MENAGERIE

Splendid are the things you've seen, *ustad*.
Every manner of flora and fauna has been
under your watchful eye.
Your supple brush brings them to life,
So that they may live anew on canvas.
The birds convene their yearly conference.
The cattle meet at the water's edge.
In the pleasure gardens,
The handmaids play.
Their sheer gowns leave little to the imagination.
Quick!
Avert your gaze before the emperor sees you.
No need to be cut down before your time.
You've far too much talent to meet an early demise.

A CARDINAL, PERHAPS

If I could decipher the language of the birds,
I'm sure they'd impart their wisdom upon me.
A much-needed push down the Path of Life,
Wherein I'm not stumbling around blindly
(I trust their sense of direction).
Yet even now,
How like a bird I feel.
The cardinal, perhaps,
Who, like his religious namesake,
Questions and ponders everything before him.
For better or for worse,
A skeptic of the highest order.

NIGHT SCENE IN YOSHIWARA

after Oi Katsushika

I walk among the throng of fishmongers and
soba peddlers in old Edo.
The River Sumida carries its life's blood
through the capital,
Veins sprawling in every conceivable direction.
The man with the dragon tattoo offers me a warm
smile.
I know what he wants,
So I switch to the opposite side of Ryōgoku Bridge.
The carts raise quite a row,
But it's to Yoshiwara they're all headed with their
lavish wares and foods.

The girls are on display,
Their painted faces catch the light.
Silk kimonos draped over their shoulders suggest the
tender flesh hidden from view.
Somewhere,
A shamisen plays.
Look how she dances,
Her fans a kaleidoscopic blur of colors.
She winks at the men,
Who breathe hard in reply.
She is, indeed, enticing.
But this is the place to forget one's troubles,
Which is why I walk this noisy street
with my eyes on the stars and nothing else.

ARCADIA

If I stay still while lying in the grass,
Perhaps I'll wither away.
The green blades will protrude from my ribcage,
Pink flowers poke through my unseeing eyes.
The insects, too, will have their feast,
More than their fair share of flesh.
To become one with the Earth is the ultimate goal,
Whether we like it or not.
It's a fate that awaits us all.
'Hereafter.'
What does it mean to me?
To rejoin the soil and into the arms of my God,
Such comfort in my final moments.

Part Two: Summer

"But we were lost in a way, didn't you feel that? The bed was like a raft; I felt us drifting far from our natures, toward a place where we'd discover nothing."

--Louise Glück, Summer

SOLSTICE

They depart for parts unknown,
Leaving me here to meditate on the nature of being.
Otherwise,
It's utter pandemonium wherein the people get too close and try to cop a feel while the pagans worship the sun.
I'm not suited for such things.
I choose, instead, to vanish into the wilderness and transcribe my verse onto a maple leaf,
My blood the ink,
My words straight from the heart.

BLACK WIDOW

I see your scarlet hourglass hanging from the rafter.
You sit in silence,
Patiently waiting for your prey.
What knowledge have you of insignificant things?
It's a question of survival,
Nothing more,
Which is why I feel remorse for the hapless moth,
Yet realize you have to make a living, too.

THE MADMAN OF AUVERS

for Vincent van Gogh

Sometimes,
The loneliness becomes unbearable.
The silence buzzes around in my mind
like a swarm of gnats.
My finger traces the moonlit landscape.
I long to be a part of it,
To feel its rhythm in my veins.
I lay my head down to sleep,
Only to have the tears flow freely.

CHAPULTEPEC

The Grasshopper rises from the lake,
Its white back catching the midday sun
like the snows of Piz Palü.
Have I woken in this alpine hell where
the stifling heat makes one sterile?
(I mean that in the creative sense).
The *calaveras* mock me from each vendor's
cart,
Their jawbones clacking away to the tempo
of my retreating footsteps.
It's Day of the Dead and I feel it too,
When a woman passes me,
Her Aztec silhouette set against a cameo glass
afternoon,
Leading her children as a mother duck does her
brood.
The sign reads: 'This way to the Temple of the Sun.'
No thanks.
I could just lie down right here and let it roast me
alive,
Baptism by fire for all the sins I've committed.
Won't you leave a poor sinner be?

THE CRICKET (A HAIKU)

The cricket outside
my window sings me to sleep
on a night in June.

BEHIND THE DUGOUT

There's something barbarous about the cry
that rises from the stands.
So primal,
So ancient.
It calls to mind gladiators or chariot races.
But here,
Everyone's a Caesar,
A Nero,
And they show their approval accordingly,
Be it a swift clap of the hands or else with
rhythmic chants,
As old as athletics themselves.

A broader democratic vista I've never seen.
Here,
The father dances with his son.
There,
The mother cheers with her daughter.
Two brothers,
Overwrought with excitement,
Behold the verdant field with wide-eyed wonder.
No doubt it's reminiscent of the stickball they'd play
together on hot summer days,
When the city felt as if it were a self-contained universe.
Such prowess on full display,
Though hard to see through the sea of straw hats.

DANCE OF THE FIREFLIES

Green flecks of light
Rise from the wet grass.
They dance in the glow of distant lightning,
A graceful,
Elegant waltz.

IN A PLAZA IN SEVILLA

In a plaza in Sevilla,
I saw a trio of *gitanos* playing a simple song.
The man strummed away at his guitar,
Caressing it as if it were a lover,
While the woman beside him sang words older
than the hills of Andalusía.

But the maiden who danced was in a trance,
Her feet and hands hypnotizing as she told a story
of love and loss.

Oh *gitanos*,
You know the world better than I,
Have seen its wonders and know its mysteries as well
as its suffering,
Which is why you play here to soothe the hearts of the
afflicted,
Offering comfort and solace to passersby.

CALAIS CROSSING

The Britannic breeze gives way to the free air
of France.
It's just a slide down Fénéon's satyr-like beard
to the land the Gauls call home.
I spare a passing thought to Charlie Parker,
The mad saxophonist of Kansas City,
Who went up the California Coast to convalesce,
Never to return.
And I see you,
Walt Whitman,
As I see those of generations hence,
Standing at the bow of this proud ferryboat that
carries its precious human cargo from the Land of
the Living to Eternity's gate.

FRIDAY AFTERNOON

My third eye opens.
It focuses on a spot on the ceiling as
Greek Orthodox chants fill my soul
with holiness.
I remember the Mediterranean,
Blue sapphire on the map,
Wedged between Europe and Africa.
Perhaps it's naïve to think it's better
elsewhere but,
When you're a dreamer,
The There is always better than Here.

NEON TIDE (BIOLUMINESCENT PLANKTON)

By day,
The sea turns to blood but,
By night,
The moon dips its milky rays into the
frothing foam,
Where they wash up on the shore like
the unfulfilled dreams of those long dead.

Fernando Pessoa digs his toes into the sand,
Holding onto his hat so it doesn't blow away.
The era of Portuguese exploration may be over,
But not for him.
He who watches everything with soulful eyes
that never waver.
Nothing escapes his gaze,
Even if it's his desires that are being swept out
to sea.

THE JINN'S PLEA

Beware, Aladdin.
I implore you to choose your wishes wisely.
Think not of yourself,
But of the greater good,
For the world suffers immensely right now.
Act kindly to others and you'll be rewarded,
Both in this life and the next.

LIBERTY LEADING THE PEOPLE

after Eugène Delacroix

Marie Antoinette hides the children of France
in her hair,
But it's too late.
No sooner does her powdered wigged head roll
do they tumble,
Like building blocks,
Onto the ground.
Their faces are African masks carved from ivory,
Ebony and palm.
No one can read what they're thinking or feeling.
Just a fixed expression that can't be cracked.

And just like that,
The monarchy has fallen!
Self-righteous peasants pillage Versailles,
Stripping the walls and gardens bare,
Entitled (so they say) to their share of the loot.
But who watches over them?
Was it not they who clamored for freedom?
What Hell is this that they've wrought upon us and,
What's more,
What does it mean?

JERUSALEM

I got drunk in the Old City,
With all my ancestors watching.
The ghost of Zoot Sims,
God rest him,
Led a march of the righteous into the
Promised Land.
All the while,
My head was swimming in Israeli wine.
The things one misses when under its spell!
Just ask Dylan Thomas,
Poor soul who was cut down too soon,
'Cause he couldn't separate life from art.

EXCAVATION AT NAXOS

A simple stone head turned gracefully
to the left,
Eyes downcast,
Hands clasped in adoration.
Just who was this stunning man,
Whose likeness was lovingly immortalized
in marble?

What drove the sculptor to create such a
masterpiece?
Maybe it was love,
Physical or unrequited,
Struck by his nude form,
Silhouetted against the moonlight.

In his prime,
He was perfection,
Yet here he lies,
His body in ruin,
But his beauty forever intact.

MILES DAVIS

I firmly plant myself on the Queens
Expressway,
Unyielding to the rush hour traffic.
Corral all your feelings into an enclosure
at the Bronx Zoo.
Delirium tremens has me seeing pink elephants
everywhere as I sit,
Washed up,
In the nauseating neon glow of a Mexican restaurant
in Berlin.
Wo weilest du?
Check, please.
With that, I'm gone,
Back up the street to the barracks I call home,
No more than a fading promise on anyone's lips.

SPICE MARKET, SAMARKAND

The stalls are as timeless as the city
itself.
Merchants and princes have walked
these very alleys.
I half expect to see Genghis Khan
downing a glass of yak's milk with his buddies.
Fragrant and mild as my temperament is in this
moment,
The spices are piled high in colorful mounds.
Earth's bounty for sale!
Best prices in town!

FUCK THE POLIS

Pericles lies in a heap on the Capitol's steps.
Dressed in rags,
He pleads,
Begging for a handout.
But Chairman Mao and Joseph Stalin take turns
kicking him into the ground.
Nothing like beating a man when he's already
down...

Someone's called the riot squad!
Cowards in masks storm the streets as all of
America burns.
The Statue of Liberty shakes her head.
She can't imagine how we've been led astray.
Her torch's flame has burned out,
The beacon of hope extinguished.

But it isn't time to throw in the towel,
To wave the white flag of surrender.
We must remain vigilant.
To the last man,
We stand,
For freedom is worth the uphill battle.

MOKSHA IN VARANASI

Saraswati compels me to write,
But I don't know what to say.
Seated on the ghats that lead down to the river,
I decide to let the city speak for me:

The cleric calls the faithful to prayer.
His voice proclaims God's glory over the rooftops
to the tune of a thousand rickshaws below.
The sun's a luminous disk in the western sky.
Like life itself,
It bears down on us like the burden of Atlas,
Yet it's through fire that we can purge ourselves
and break the chain of rebirth.

City of Shiva.
Funny how the bringer of destruction can also merit
the creation of something beautiful.

At the end of the day,
I pay my quarter to the ferryman,
Who delivers me to *moksha* on the opposite shore.
He offers me a missing-toothed grin.
He too is holy,
As all the people here are holy.
Kadosh, kadosh, kadosh!
Shanti.

BACK TO BROOKLYN, 4:00 AM

John Coltrane and Cannonball Adderley
talk to each other through the stereo.
I listen intently.
The lilts in their conversation,
The strides in their tone make for an
intimate affair.
I'm an impartial observer,
A voyeur,
Yet my ears simply can't turn away.
With the rattle and hum of each passing
railcar on the Williamsburg Bridge,
The universe of my consciousness expands
in an explosion of color behind me,
A cartoon thought bubble that reveals a lot
about me and what makes this body and mind tick.

Ah, strangers!
Drunken NYU undergrads in expensive coats
and luxurious scarves.
If they make eye contact,
They're looking for action,
But I'm too wrapped up in my own world,
Like the beauty of a former Dutch colony at the edge
of existence
On a night like tonight that's seemingly endless in the
best possible way.

WHERE THE SHADOW MEN ARE

It's just around the bend to the place
where the shadow men are.
They hide among the trees,
Lust-filled eyes peering through the leaves
to scan the road for their next victim.
It isn't so often they get to whet their appetites,
Though they're truly exquisite,
A gallery of taut skin and hard bodies.

AN OASIS

I remember exactly how it was:
Stoic,
As in an afternoon's golden splendor.
The columns of date palms hold up the sky
like an ancient temple to some long-forgotten deity.
In their shade,
The silhouette of a farmer holding court with Gilgamesh.
How reminiscent,
This mirage,
Of a land between two rivers,
The fertile heart of the Judean Desert.
We listen intently,
The farmer and I,
To the Ancient One's Sumerian song.
It trills like a boat on the water,
With its many crests and waves.
Green parrots overhead add a verse or two,
Hidden within the fronds.

LONDON DOUBLE-DECKER

It's a metaphysical journey,
A transformation,
That takes place between Trafalgar Square
and Downing Street.
A tenacious people walk these streets,
A proud race.
I can feel every drop of hot August air on my body.
The wind off the Thames hits my face and I've never
felt freer,
Like I'm soaring over the battlements of Newgate
Prison,
To a wider world,
Somewhere far away.

Part Three: Autumn

"Then leaf subsides to leaf.
So Eden sank to grief,
So dawn goes down today,
Nothing gold can stay."
–Robert Frost, Nothing Gold Can Stay

FIRST DAY OF FALL

I lose myself amongst the reeds.
The water here is shallow,
And to float along is to take flight upon
the afternoon's many treasures.
The glories of July and August have passed
me by,
As have September's promises,
Yet here I lie,
Well content,
So long as this blissful moment lasts forever.

CENSORED

The flaming horse breaks free!
It loosens itself from its tethers
and escapes the carousel when
no one's watching.
Speeding down the highway,
It heads with leaps and bounds
from Central Park to the asylum
at Camarillo,
Where I'm paying Holden Caulfield
a visit.

He asks about the weather.
Useless small talk.
What else can you say when you're
confined to a loony bin?
I leave flowers at his bedside,
Praying they don't wilt before he has
the chance to enjoy them.
He's broken and bruised,
Another victim of the system that calls
for unnecessary censorship.

Outside,
The flaming horse is doused with water.
Every dream we've ever had is crushed.
'Burn down the libraries,'
The people shout,
For it's their endeavor to make us all as
miserable as they are.
They thrive in a world of unhappiness and
their reality,
In turn,
Becomes everyone's.

SISYPHUS IN HELL

Such is life, my friend:
Pushing dreams to the edge of the summit,
Only to have them fall and shatter.

THOUGHTS RACING

It's hard to keep up.
They race down the superhighway
at breakneck speed.
Head in hands,
I clutch my hair and let out an animal cry
that'd chill any wild beast to the bone.
Darkness,
Darkness abounds.
It swallows me up like a great whale,
The plight of Jonah right there,
Out in the open.
Why do tears sting?
Because the scars they leave behind run deep,
Deeper than we could ever imagine.

OCTOBER CHILL

The air has a bite to it.
It foretells of winter with its snow and ice.
It smells like memories that aren't my own.
I could search from County Cork to the East Coast
and everywhere in between.
No peace I find would compare to this.

PAPERBACK

When I close my eyes,
I recall him distinctly.
The shape of him appears
out of the darkness,
Completely unchanged by the
intervening years:

He stands on a corner of the
Emerald City,
Green eyes concealed behind
tinted shades.
Red flannel hugs his form tightly.
I can trace each muscle with my
hungry gaze.

But his most distinctive feature:
A paperback book (Kerouac's
Dharma Bums) juts out of his back
left pocket like a faithful companion.
He notices me staring and shakes
the blond locks out of his face.

For the briefest of moments,
We're the only two people on Earth,
Two lost souls who've found each other
through the ether of life,
Mad for a taste of the fruit which,
For far too long,
We've been told is forbidden.

COLCHIS

Somewhere in the doldrums that
surround London lies the entrance
to the spirit world.
In an elegant pub I sit,
Nursing my fourth Guinness.
I see the shades and specters pass by
outside at time-lapse speed.
D'you think they know they're ghosts?
I press the cold glass to my reddened brow
and wonder when the vision will subside.

THE PARKING LOT COUNCIL

Just four guys in a parking lot,
The Four Horsemen of the Apocalypse,
Shootin' the shit and commenting on the
aches and pains of life.
For an instant,
Just us against the whole of creation,
A mere blip in the cosmic fabric.
But it was everything to us 'cause,
For the briefest of moments,
It was as it had been before.

IN THE CROCODILE'S MOUTH

I took ayahuasca in Auvers to see
what it was the madmen saw.
I wandered into that place where the
briar grows wild and stung my eyes
with the thorns.
I thought my heart was full but,
As it turns out,
It was completely empty,
Having been wrung of all emotion.
Just as the butterfly isn't meant to be caged,
So I'm not meant to be imprisoned in the
padded cell of life.
And my hollow self laid prone in the wheat fields,
Observing a night sky painted with strange shapes.

JERSEY CITY, ACROSS THE RIVER

To what are you reaching skyward?
I know your storied past,
Know that a not-so-elder statesman
was shot and killed on your sacred ground.
Only back East can so great a city be this close
to another,
Flavored with exotic Dutch and Lenape names:
Bergen, Weehawken, Secaucus.
What do you make of your aspirations?
At one doorstep,
The jeweled city.
At the other,
The spoils of the continent.
To which will you reveal your true intentions?

TO EDGAR ALLAN POE

I'm trying not to crack.
The raven on my windowsill is
a constant reminder of my mortality.
Fear grips my mind in a sort of vice,
Inflating it like a balloon that could burst
at any moment.
A great many thoughts weigh heavy
on my conscience,
A burden no mortal man could easily bear.

KAMIYAMA

The haiku feeds the waters of an ancient stream.
I walk in the footsteps of the gods.
It's Valhalla,
Olympus.
The divinity is the same.
How Moses felt in the presence of the Lord,
That selfsame ecstasy makes my very heart leap
with joy.
There is no loneliness when love is all around us.
We become a part of something bigger than ourselves,
A bridge between the physical realm and eternity.
The crane understands this spirituality,
Which is why he bows as he walks.
Good fortune smiles upon the pilgrims who've made
the trek from the edge of the world to Paradise.
Make no mistake:
We may look different but,
At the end of the day,
We all strive for the same thing.

THE FOX AND THE RAVEN

Once the woods have cleared
and the full moon begins its flight
across the cosmic ocean,
The fox and the raven emerge from
their hiding places
To make a little mischief.

'Bring out the cauldron,'
The fox commands.
'And I'll collect the ingredients.'
A half-hour later,
They reconvene in a clearing
they've trampled out themselves.

With a squawk of delight,
The raven lights the fire
While the fox adds the sprigs and leaves
he's gathered to the mixture.
Black smoke rises,
Obscuring the moonlight,
And spreads throughout the globe.

Chaos ensues.
Thunder and lightning!
Mankind turns on one another.
The fox and the raven cackle with glee
at the mayhem they've caused.
They simply can't rest until there's a ruckus.

Some say the pair are still in that spot,
Dancing 'round the stoked flames like the
heathens they are,
Celebrating the misfortune they've wrought.
When will their hunger be satisfied?

NOVEMBER

Like the turning of a page,
October gives way to November and,
With it,
Comes an inexplicable somberness.
Perhaps it's the changing of the seasons
from hot to cold.
The evening air is rich with the fragrance
of decaying leaves.
They crunch beneath our shoes along with
the dashed hopes of many a wasted day.
Even the moon,
Rising in the East,
Looks sad,
Her celestial consorts a procession
of funeral mourners to commemorate the glories
of summer.
Tomb eternal,
Let not these wasted tears water the earth.
To see what lies on the horizon is,
By far,
The greatest blessing at the end of the year.

LANGSTON HUGHES IN MEXICO

It was in a darkened cantina
That I heard a mariachi sing
'The Weary Blues.'
He put his heart and soul into it,
Calling on both the *cante jondo*
of his Spanish ancestors as well as
the tribal chants of his Aztec forbears.
The scene formed a triptych I'll never forget,
With Heaven,
Purgatory and Hell illuminated as in a Biblical
manuscript,
The imps crawling from the bottle of *anis*
into my glass with relative ease.
Mischief-makers.
They're more trouble than they're worth.
And in my delirium,
I swat them away like mosquitos in a summer night's
fever dream.

CONSTRUCTION CRANE AT DUSK

It stands like a prehistoric relic
from a time long before man.
When the hard-hats have retired
for the day,
It roosts,
A sauropod dinosaur made of steel,
Its long neck bent in prayer,
As if to thank the earth god for its bounty.

EVENING REFRAIN

Sometimes to stave off loneliness,
I pay my friends, the shadows,
A visit,
Knowing full well that they'll be home.
The first drag of that cigarette fills my lungs
with warmth.
A memory pops into my head of younger days,
When everything seemed brighter.
Funny how the colors fade the older you get.
Once I reach the railroad tracks,
There's no turning back.
The midnight train to Watsonville's due any minute.
Boxcar thoughts whisk me away to those
strawberry fields,
A promised land of fertile valleys.

California dreamin' has become the California
nightmare.
It's a precarious situation,
To experience the decline of society.
Some have taken to idol worship,
But nothing good comes from bowing before
the fatted calf.
Like the citizens of Sodom and Gomorrah,
I'd rather be transformed into a pillar of salt
When all is said and done.

DYLAN

Son of the sea,
Itinerant bard
Born and raised in the Breadbasket
of America.
All you've known is peace (nothing of war).
I tell you,
Be grateful for that.
He gets high on the vapors of factory
smokestacks
And knows nothing but his own reality,
Which he mirrors back to us on ivory skin
and a rosy complexion.

LACRIMOSA

Picture a young man in the throes of war,
Furiously etching his pain onto whatever
scraps of paper he can find.
Around him,
The shell-blasts of his insecurities burst forth,
Ripping his soul to shreds.
It's enough to drive the strongest of men to madness.
At the end of another battle-weary day,
He succumbs to his grief and lays in an open field,
Carrion birds pecking at his still-warm flesh.

CAN'T

I can't stand the silence,
Can't handle noise,
Can't tolerate judgment from the girls and boys.
I can't bear the bad news,
Can't handle stress,
Can't suffer this pain that I feel in my chest.
I can't endure struggle.
The times can be hard,
But I wonder what happens if I pull out *that* card.
Maybe things'll be better
For all those involved,
For all of my problems this answer will solve.

But no…

I *can* handle silence.
It's all in my head.
The peace that comes to me when I go to bed
Is a welcome reprieve
From the noise of the day,
Back when I wished it would all go away.
And I know who to thank,
I know that it's true,
But more than myself,
I owe it to you.

THE BALLAD OF MARK DAVID CHAPMAN

He heard the music in his head
when he shot John Lennon dead.
Holden Caulfield he was not,
But that's not what *he* thought.

It was a brisk December day
when he stepped out of the fray.
With a pistol in his hand,
He cautiously approached the man.

'Hey man,'
He said with a quiver in his voice.
He knew he had a choice.
But when he took another step,
Lennon knew and his heart leapt.

With a bang,
The pistol fired.
And with that,
Lennon retired to a place with golden fields
where peace and love no longer yield.
Just death and darkness all throughout.
Ain't no way Chapman's ever getting out.

There was no music in his head
when he shot John Lennon dead.

THE RECKONING

Contort the mind.
Stretch it to the limit to adopt
the polluted mindset of the
present age,
Where up is down,
Right is wrong,
And evil masquerades as benevolence.
Some call it the Reckoning.
Others refer to it as the alignment
of the planets.
Whatever your belief,
It's here.
We stand at a crossroads,
Where the road not taken stares us down,
Urging us toward its path.
It's up to us,
What we decide.
But given our history,
Will we make the right decision?
The poet waits with bated breath,
His pen poised to chronicle all,
To immortalize it in language that stings,
Yet always tells the truth.

Part Four: Winter

"The sight is lost in an opaque, thick haze.
No sign of the stars: They no longer blaze!
The eyes see no more—but one step ahead;
We pass silent and somber with our tumbling
tread."

--Mehdi Akhavan Sales, Winter

BACK TO THE WASTELAND

The creek has run dry.
In its bed,
The stones lie bleached and baked
in the midday sun,
Bones of a long dead giant.
Up on the hillside,
A parched tree stretches its arms to the heavens
in a last-ditch effort to beg for mercy.
Kraken of the grassland,
Your sorry state mirrors my own.
In a stagnant environment,
How can anything hope to survive?
My mind draws blanks,
The hollowed-out ruins of an old sanctuary,
Remnant of a civilization that once thrived.
It's a sorry state.
Even the raven wants nothing to do with me.
Cackling as she goes,
She feasts on what's left of my skin.
Prometheus,
Where have you gone?
Has the fire you so compassionately gifted us
burned out at last?
We all knew this day was coming.
It was just a matter of when.
And now,
Ill prepared,
We're forced to face it.

PERSEPHONE

Scrap the blueprint.
I'm going to build my heart from scratch.
That way,
No one or nothing can break it.
I stare into the dark recesses of the caldera,
Recalling the times when they'd sacrifice
virgins to the volcano.
Ah,
Glory be to the days of old!
Surely such barbarism was the sign of a
superior age,
Right?
Tilt the lens so I can see more clearly.
Rose-colored glasses make everything seem
brighter.
The optics of Harun al-Rashid simply can't
compare.
When the devil comes to whisk you away,
What will you do then?
I'll stand idly by,
As you did,
Engrossed by how things should be,
But aren't.

KRIEG (WAR)

From Thermopylae to Mosul,
The virus has infected every corner
of the globe.
Sometimes it's necessary,
To stop evil in its tracks.
But more often than not,
Those afflicted are mere pawns
in an immense chess game played by gods
(or else faceless men) in an office in some
far-flung capital.
Let not their blood satisfy the morbid appetites
of Flanders Fields,
Nor the flesh-strewn jungles of Vietnam.
Grant them the strength and fortitude to live on,
Despite the things they carry.

RIMBAUD IN NEW ORLEANS

The absinthe kicks in
And I stumble out into the balmy evening
from the claustrophobia of a Bourbon Street
dive.
Framed in the greasy halo of a gas lamp,
The book in my back pocket cries out,
Calling the shots.
The clip-clop of shod hooves on the cobblestones
is the sound of my restraint being swept away by
gale-force winds.
The night is a promise of the regrets to come,
But my heart's mad for a taste of them.

FORAY INTO THE SURREAL

Whose face stares back at me
from the window's blackened reflection?
It appears as a series of shapes.
A triangle here,
An oval there,
Nothing that suggests a human being.
Perhaps that's just my psyche: broken.
But when the morning comes and the
disparate pieces fit back together again,
I wonder why I ever doubted myself.

Untitled

I never believed in Deus Ex Machina
until the time I tried to drown out my sorrows,
When each song on the radio reminded me of you.
It would appear that the universe has it in for me,
Which,
After the way I left things,
I suppose I deserve.
The language of intimacy isn't a tongue in which I'm fluent.
I could afford to brush up on it from time to time.
If you need me,
You can find me at the local watering hole,
Holding court with the poets who,
Though long dead,
Have taught me a great deal in the intervening years.

NOMADIC EXISTENCE

The Steppenwolf roams the barren plains
of Central Asia.
He's a restless spirit,
Never content to stay in one place for too long.
Nowhere and everywhere is his home.
He yearns to breathe free in this suffocating world
where timidity is for the weak.
His muzzle forms the words:
'Be outspoken!
Be heard!
For the voice of reason is so often silenced by that
of blind conformity.'

PICASSO'S BLUE PERIOD

It was the death of his friend
that put him in a bad way:
Suicide in the middle of the Rue l'Odéon.
Amid the clamor of car horns and hot jazz,
A bullet through the right temple.
The women of town merely shook their heads
forlornly,
But the painter fully mourned him.
Wiping the tears away with his brush,
He attacked the canvas with broad strokes
to mirror the pain in his heart.
So it was that,
Drenched in blue,
He conducted his masterful symphony,
Leaving not a dry eye in the house.

POLAR BEAR

Queen of the North,
I see your face a thousand times
in a dewdrop chandelier,
Backlit by the winter moon.
Killing machine,
Each muscle and sinew are taut
and ready to spring.
Your inner fire drives you forward.
You act on instinct,
Eyes glowing red,
Breath like smoke issues from your
powerful jaws.
O great dragon of the frozen tundra,
Cast your gaze skyward and let the aurora
christen you anew.
Her green veils will bathe you in holiness.
Only then can you protect your brood,
Proudest offspring of a savage race.

SATURNALIA

Swimming in a moonlit stream,
We watch as the pearls dance off
our fingertips.
Through the blue window,
Grey clouds pass in a flicker,
But none of it matters,
For I'm lost in the desire of his eyes,
And nothing could tear me away from
the present moment,
The sweet here and now that I wish
would never end.

ANATOMY OF THE POET

I now know why Orpheus sings,
Why the poets weep in the night.
It's more out of necessity than
anything else,
For they carry a burden unlike
any other:
The weight of the world,
Set to music in a symphony of joy
and sorrow.
Who wouldn't be able to control themselves
under such circumstances?
That's why we've got to sing.
Otherwise,
We'd die.
It's like breathing or a heartbeat,
An involuntary part of our biology.

A NIGHT IN TUNISIA

A series of jagged shapes appears
within the hookah smoke.
Is it an elephant or a camel?
The girl behind the bar,
Who's fluent in the language of
crocodiles,
Eyes me suspiciously.
She must've been burned by my kind
before.
In the corner,
A sheikh tells tales of the desert,
How it once was and its many mysteries.
We gather 'round him,
Spellbound,
Sewn into the intricate tapestry he weaves.

METAMORPHOSE

When I dream,
My head detaches itself
from the rest of my body
and embarks to points unknown.
It passes the factories where clouds
are made and through seas of sand
that have swallowed ships whole.
From such stark imagery,
My mind gathers meaning,
Though it takes time to materialize,
Much like the insect within a chrysalis.

THE SLOWEST MONTH

January is the slowest month.
It crawls by at a snail's pace.
See the bored clergy in the churches
and synagogues,
Debating amongst themselves the meaning
of God's word,
All to empty pews.
In abandoned warehouses,
The dancers huddle together for warmth,
A sensual *pas-de-deux*.
Their glistening,
Twisting bodies form into a single entity,
A ghastly creature of entwined arms and legs,
One whose movements will forecast the morale
of the coming year with skill and foresight.

SPIRIT OF '76

The fifes have taken their last breaths.
They collapse in a heap on the blood-soaked
earth.
The drums of war fall silent,
The drummers having been riddled with bullets.
Only the flag-bearer remains.
With tears in his eyes and love in his heart,
He storms into the fray with quiet dignity,
Only to be cut down in his prime.
No one mourns.
No one weeps.
Instead,
They celebrate,
Taking to the streets and trampling on the memory
of those who came before.
(Fickle creatures they are.
They turn at the drop of a hat).
Will no one remember them?
Honor their memory?
If not,
We're fated to become another cautionary tale,
A mere footnote in the annals of history.
Who will celebrate our greatness?
Let the poets speak for us,
To give voice,
As they so often do,
To the voiceless.

SUBURBIA

I send my love through the power lines,
Hoping that it reaches you.
Silhouetted against the green hills,
The pylons hum,
Carrying my pulse in their wires.
Be careful,
For the cargo you bear is precious
and should reach the intended unscathed.

NOSTALGIA (DUAL HAIKUS)

Nostalgia is a form of time travel,
But why is it so often accompanied by feelings of
melancholy?

ONE YEAR ON

The church bells have fallen silent
and the streets are all deserted.
Where have the happy people gone?
Indoors or underground,
Never again to be roused from their
slumber.
It's an eerie feeling,
Navigating this city I once knew,
When all I hear are the sound of my
thoughts
As well as my broken heart.

DAWN/DUSK

Things always appear clearest in the dawn.
The sea resuscitates me with her salty kisses.
Like her,
They're limitless.
A peacock crows.
Eyes on its tail blink in unison,
As if they can read my soul.
Gently he wades into the surf,
Unaware of the sacrifice he's making.
Should I stop him?
Such beauty need not be wasted,
But these chains are holding me back.
Samson,
Bring this cliffside down if you wish to see
your love again.
To be eyeless in Gaza is a fate worse than death.

The twilight hour is always marked by the lighting
of the first lantern.
See how the houses appear like ghosts in the night's
encroaching darkness.
Familiar as the streets may be,
This isn't the place of my childhood,
For it has assumed a desolate air.
I breathe it in,
Feeling how it burns my lungs.
But one hit's all it takes,
And I'm back to the start so I can see where it is
that I went wrong.

NEIGHBORHOOD CONVERSATIONS

In the shade of the open garage door,
Two men,
One old,
One young,
Talk animatedly in English and Vietnamese.
So quickly do they switch from one to the other
that I can hardly keep track.
Across the way,
The aromatic scent of cooked meat makes the dogs
salivate.
Four men and a woman bemoan the previous night's game:
'So-and-so's defense is shit.'
'Did you see that play?
Fuckin' brutal,'
Yet they laugh at the ridiculousness of it all.
Their laughter cuts through the hedges and reaches my ears,
Which perk up instinctively.
To know the neighborhood's alive and well fills me with
so much joy,
Yet I'm always on its fringes,
A constant impartial observer.
Such detachment might trouble the average person but,
To me,
It's merely second nature.

THE VEIL

Beyond the veil,
What does she see?
A new world,
Perhaps,
With endless possibilities?
Or maybe a trick of the light,
A figure in the darkened hallway
she hadn't noticed before.
The golden stars gleam on sheer
blue silk,
A galaxy of dreams she wraps herself in
whenever reality rears its ugly head.

Made in the USA
Columbia, SC
10 January 2024